Jospeh
HAYDN

TRUMPET CONCERTO
Hob.VIIe: 1
(1796)

Edited by
Clark McAlister

Study Score
Partitur

SERENISSIMA MUSIC, INC.

ORCHESTRA

2 Flutes

2 Oboes

2 Bassoons

2 Horns in E-flat

2 Trumpets in E-flat

Timpani

Violin I

Violin II

Viola

Violoncello

Bass

Duration: ca.15 minutes
First performance: March 28, 1800
Vienna
Anton Weidinger, keyed trumpet
Imperial Court Orchestra

© Copyright 2010 Clark McAlister.
All rights reserved.

This study score is an unabridged reprint – in reduced format – of the large conductor's score previously issued by E. F. Kalmus as catalog number A7278. The large score and a complete set of parts are exclusively available for sale from Serenissima Music, Inc.

CONCERTO
for Trumpet and Orchestra
in E flat

JOSEPH HAYDN, H VIIe: 1

Practical Performing Edition by Clark McAlister

* Set also includes parts for Horns in F and Trumpets (including Solo) in B♭.

SERENISSIMA MUSIC, INC.

* Vc./D.B. MS has [figure] -- surely an oversight? See m. 12.
** Viola: MS indicates "Col basso" to m. 52 -- also an oversight? See m. 13.

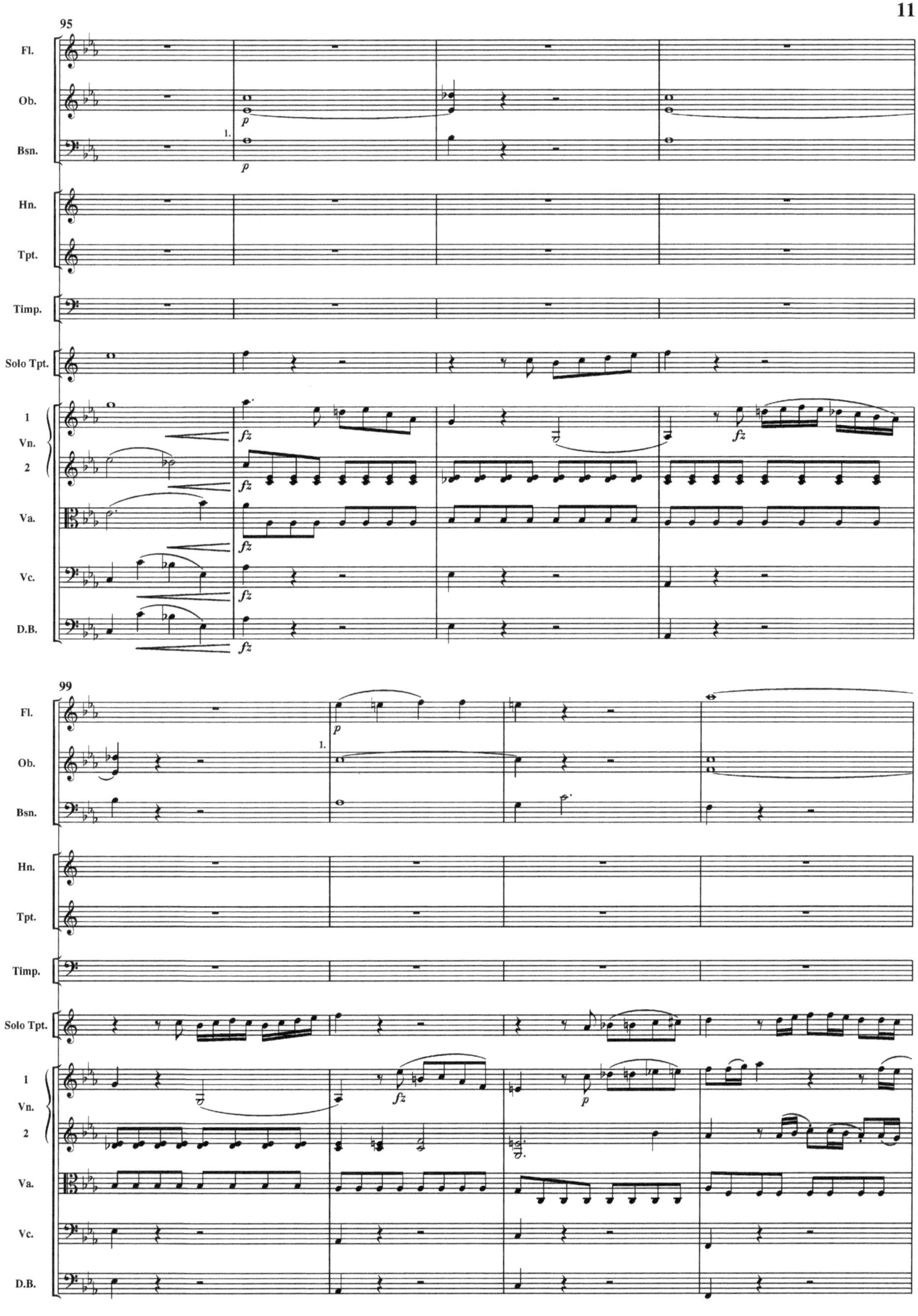

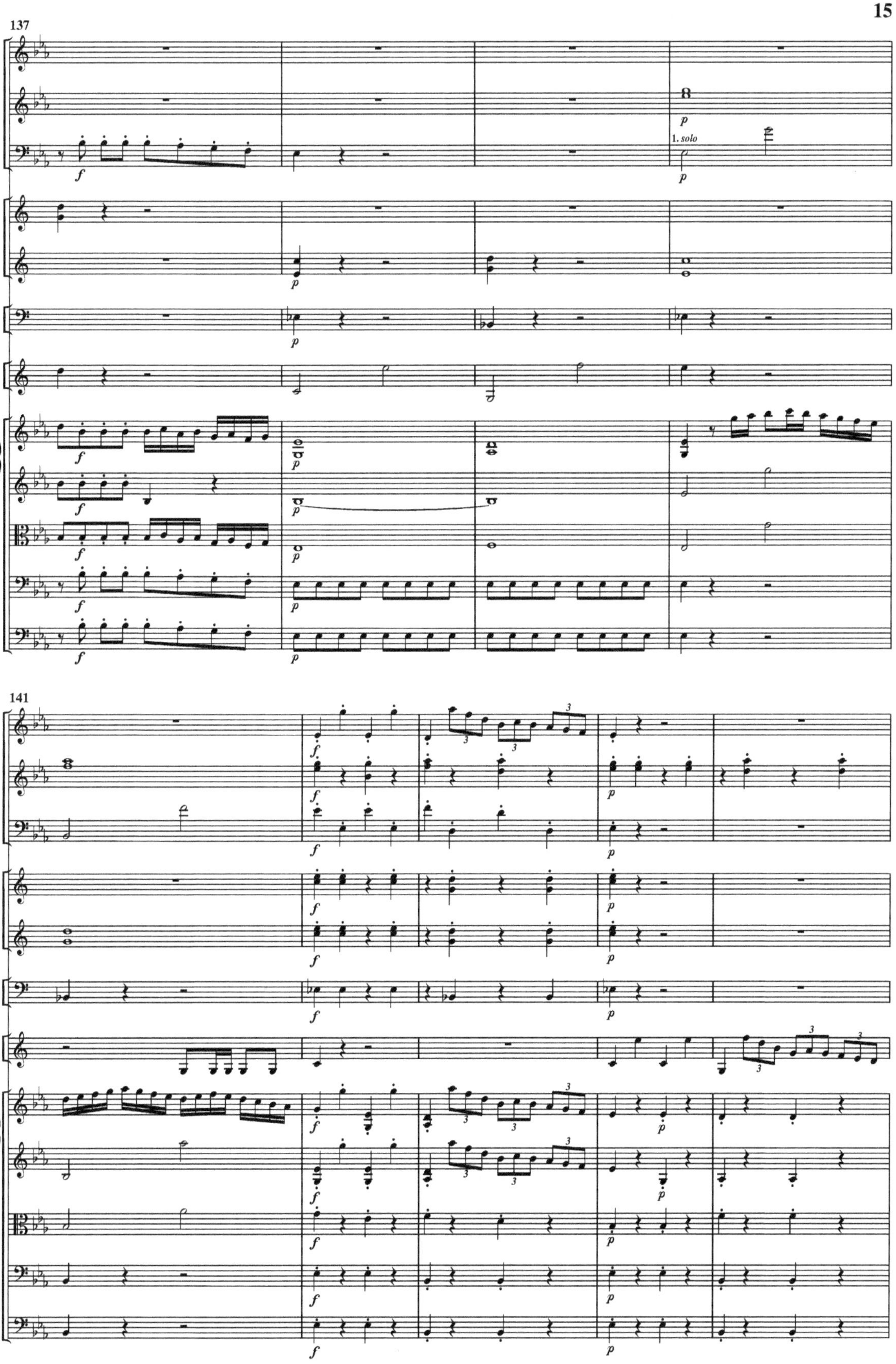
137
Fl.
Ob.
Bsn.
1. solo
Hn.
Tpt.
Timp.
Solo Tpt.
1
Vn.
2
Va.
Vc.
D.B.
141
Fl.
Ob.
Bsn.
Hn.
Tpt.
Timp.
Solo Tpt.
1
Vn.
2
Va.
Vc.
D.B.

* Haydn's MS. has this rhythm on B♭.
* MS. has ♯♯.

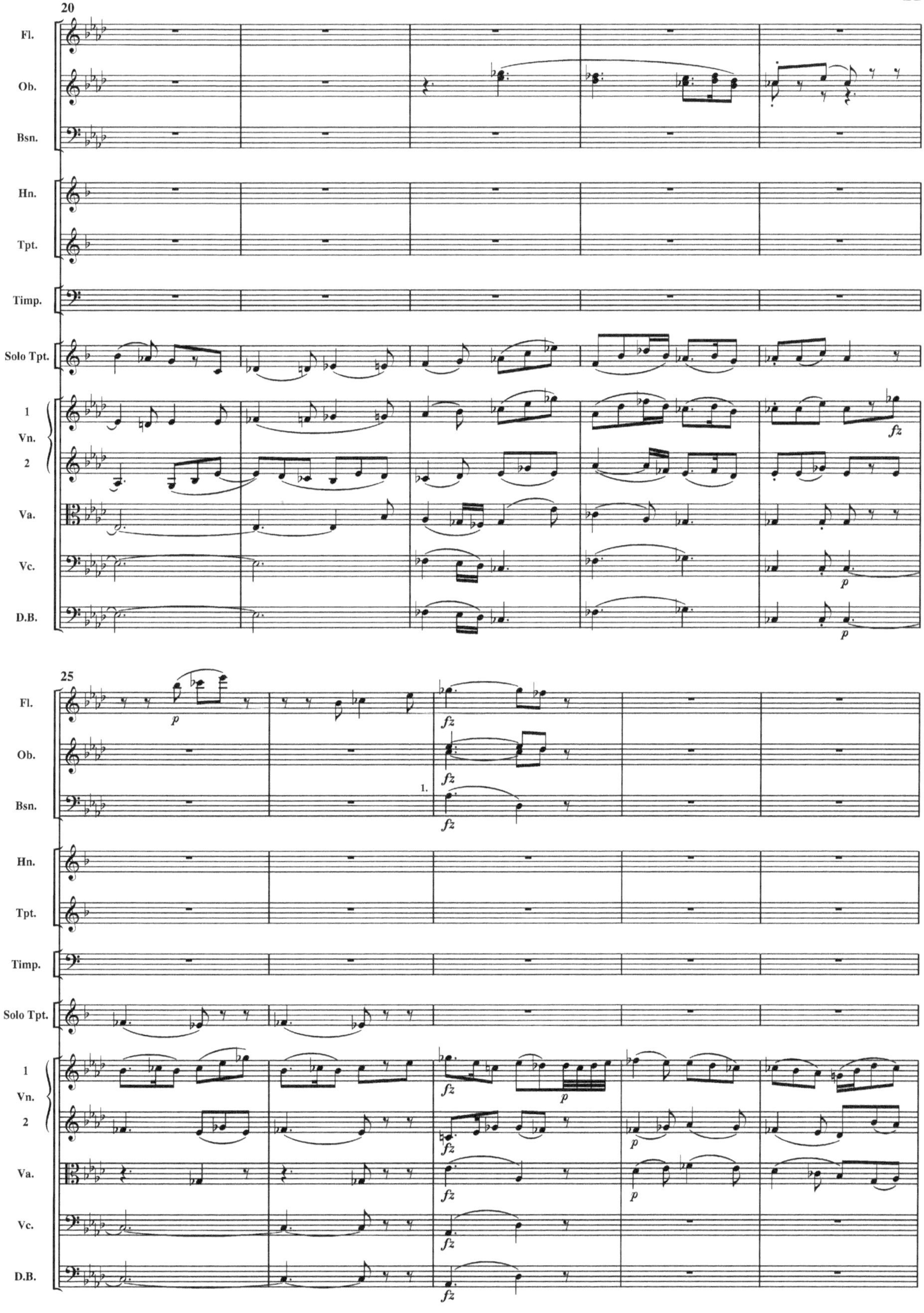
20
Fl.
Ob.
Bsn.
Hn.
Tpt.
Timp.
Solo Tpt.
1
Vn.
2
Va.
Vc.
D.B.
fz
p
25
1.

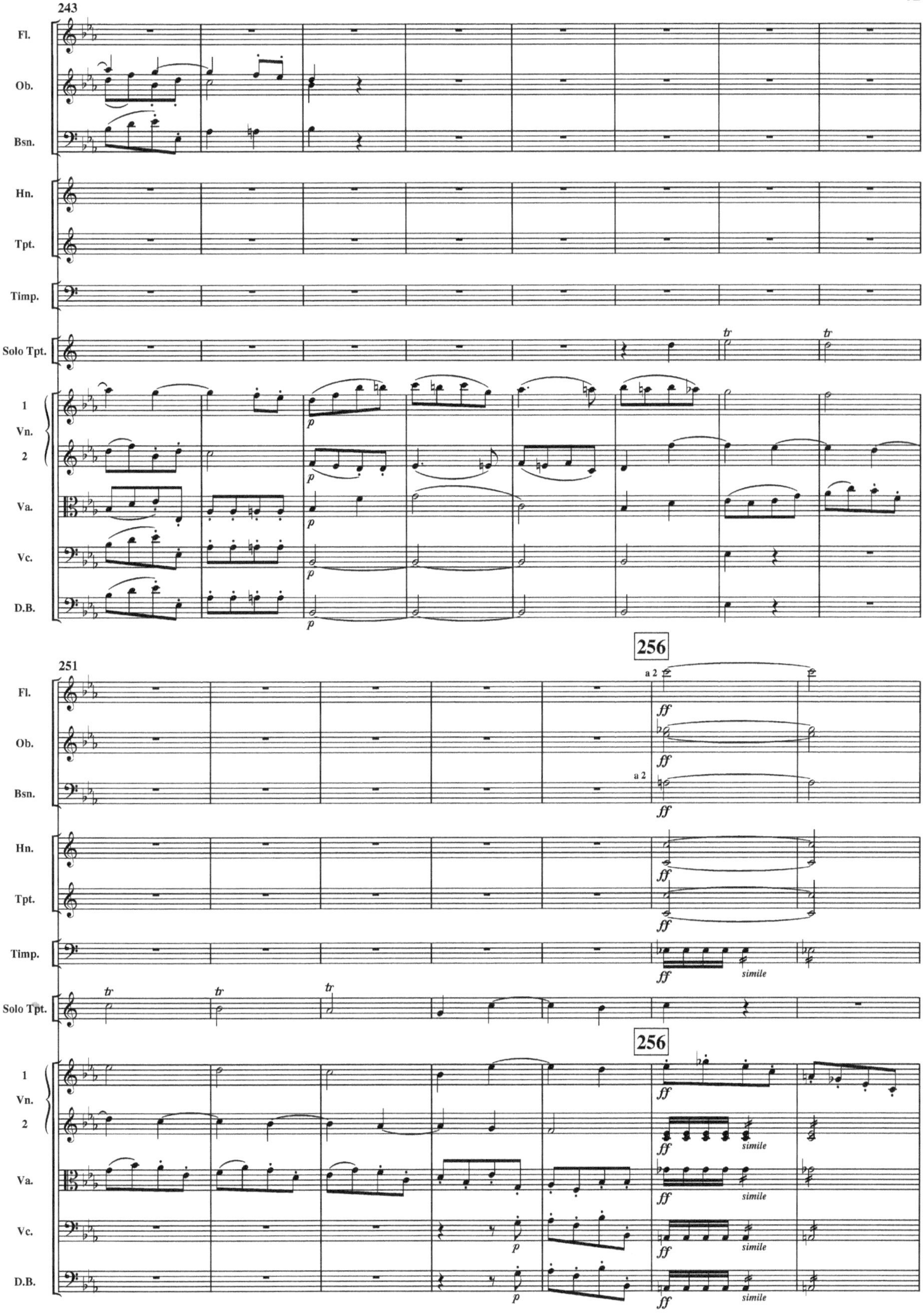
243
Fl.
Ob.
Bsn.
Hn.
Tpt.
Timp.
Solo Tpt.
1
Vn.
2
Va.
Vc.
D.B.
251
256
a 2
ff
simile
p

www.ingramcontent.com/pod-product-compliance
Lightning Source LLC
Chambersburg PA
CBHW081350040426
42450CB00015B/3386